MINDING THE BREATH

Meditation Techniques of the Anapanasati

Mindfulness of Breathing

MINDING THE BREATH

Meditation Techniques of the Anapanasati

Mindfulness of Breathing

Shane Wilson

<u>Notice of Copyright</u>

<u>Notice of Liability</u>

Printed in the United States of America

"This is how mindfulness of breathing is developed and pursued so as to be of great fruit and great benefit."

The Buddha

CONTENTS

Mindfulness of Dhammas

Acknowledgments

Several instrumental authors and teachers have had influence on this work. They and their work have easily earned the right to be mentioned here. They are; *Mindfulness with Breathing* by Buddhadasa Bhikkhu, translated by Santikaro Bhikku from Wisdom Publications; *The Middle Length Discourses of the Buddha,* translated by Bhikku Nanamoli and Bhikku Bodhi from Wisdom Publications and *Satipatthana: The Direct Path to Realization* by Analayo from Windhorse publications.

It would be completely unintentional if there where similarities in definitions or explanations found within these pages and those of other writings. There is no implied intention to borrow from others works beyond the typical information one learns through general interest and study.

It is with deep gratitude and sincerity that I can say this work would not be complete without the knowledge and effort put forth by Denise Dearborn, the editor of this book. Thank you.

Introduction

The purpose of this book is twofold. This book has been written to help the person who is new to meditation access states of calm and relaxation. Alternatively, it is meant to aid those who have already established a regular meditation practice.

By using the meditation instructions provided within the Buddhist Sutta: *"The Anapanasati"*, translated as *mindfulness with breathing*, the meditator can take their practice to any level desired. Each of the areas of this practice has a depth that can literally be practiced for ones entire lifetime without need for further instruction. However, a proper understanding and consistent practice is essential.

Remaining relevant for today's meditators, these timeless meditation instructions had been provided some 2600 years ago by the Buddha. They encompass a total of sixteen steps that many consider to be progressive. The sixteen areas are naturally categorized into four separate areas of study. These four areas of the Anapanasati are: the Body, Feelings, Mind States and Dhammas.

In this book are interpretations of the instructions from the *Anapanasati Sutta,* followed by a commentary, or explanation, of each of the sixteen areas. As we progress along the passages, there will be written, guided meditations provided in order to allow one to get a clearer idea of how to use and incorporate the meditation into their practice. It is not enough to only read and understand the sutta; one must have an actual method of practice. The guided meditations are meant to provide this.

As you do these meditations, you will likely come to the realization that these practices will be both rewarding, and for some, challenging. The meditations progress from simple instructions pertaining to the breath alone. They then move toward deeper, relational reflections concerning the activity of the mind. The instructions then progress toward the Buddhist teaching of impermanence and the true understandings of the nature of reality. During all of the sixteen steps, the breath is the primary subject, or remains as an important part, of these practices.

There are sixteen separate meditations in all, each one being unique, but still very much a part of the whole. Take your time as you work your way through this book. Its intention is to present an uncomplicated and enjoyable method of meditation practice as described by the Buddha.

The Practice of Meditation

The farmer and the buffalo

There is a story about a rice farmer who had a friendly, but untrained, water buffalo. It is not uncommon for an Asian rice farmer to become close friends with their water buffalo since they often work all day together. The strong water buffalo helps plow the fields, harvest the rice, and often provides milk for the farmer's family, as well as companionship. The farmer in this story is very kind to his buffalo. He is so kind that he did not like to tie up the buffalo with a rope when they were not working. Instead, the farmer wanted the buffalo to roam freely around the farm and eat the weeds that grew so quickly around the buildings.

Although, there was one problem, you see, water buffalos love to eat rice plants. It is food for them. The farmer was trying to grow the rice for his family to eat and to sell at the local market. So, he had to keep the buffalo away from the plants. The farmer decided to train the buffalo to stay out of the rice plants instead of tying the buffalo up with a rope.

The farmer began his buffalo training. Every time the buffalo was found near the rice plants, the farmer would gently tap the buffalo on the back with a stick and herd him away from the rice plants. This went on for many days and the farmer grew weary. He thought there must be a better way to train the buffalo to stay out of the rice plants. Then he realized something! He is not training the buffalo to 'not' go toward the rice plants! Instead, he was only training him to 'get out' of the rice plants once he was already in them.

With this awareness, the farmer decided to stay very close to the buffalo and train him properly. Every time the buffalo moved toward the rice plants, the farmer would tap him on the back with the stick. At first, it was hard to spend so much time watching the buffalo. Before long, the buffalo learned to not even move toward the rice plants. Eventually, the buffalo became so well-trained that the farmer did not have to watch him so closely. It was as if the buffalo was watching himself! Life became much easier for both the farmer and the water buffalo.

The same is true in our meditation practice. The water buffalo represents the mind. We must learn to be the watcher of the mind and keep it from wondering off toward the things to which it should not be wandering. This is just like the buffalo heading toward the rice plants.

We must be like the farmer and keep a watch on the mind. If we have patience and stay engaged with the activity of the mind, we will easily learn to notice the movements of the mind even before the movement actually happens. We saw that this was a better way to train the buffalo and the same is true when training the mind with a practice in meditation. When done in this way, we will soon see that life can become much easier.

What you can expect from this practice

Meditation is, foremost, a calming of the body. When this is accomplished, the mind follows and becomes calm as well. With the process of meditation, we learn to more easily watch the activity of the mind. As many already know, this has many benefits, both physical and mental. Many of these benefits are directly related to the decrease of stress. This decrease in stress is accomplished through this practice, first, by understanding that we create this stress ourselves. Second, we notice, through mindfulness, that we hang onto and store this stress within the body. For those that are new to meditation, when calming the body and stilling the mind, there will likely be a noticing of how the mind is mostly untrained. With a consistent practice, we learn to effortlessly be one with, and work more easily with the mind.

Very often, when we meditate, we place our attention on the breath. This gives us a place to rest our concentration. When this is done, we will soon notice that the attention that was on the breath has wandered. When we notice that it has wandered, we bring our attention back to the breath. In meditation, we do this repeatedly. To the person who does not understand the practice of meditation, this may seem to be a senseless activity. Although, as we do this, we are actually doing something that may well be the most beneficial activity anyone could possibly do! We are training the mind, as well as strengthening our concentration. This is the basis behind meditation. Why do we do this? This is done so that we can learn to calm the mind of its habitual business. This calming allows us to witness the true nature of the mind, which is "stillness". The still mind is the mind without its many unyielding thoughts. This busy, cluttered mind is not our friend and, as previously mentioned, the still mind is much easier to work with. This "stilling" of the mind also results in freedom from daily troubles, increasing our level of happiness. The personal benefits will be discovered by you, through a daily practice, as we go through the material in this book.

Concentration and mindfulness

By stilling and concentrating the mind, the answers to our questions present themselves freely. All we have to do is listen to them. The "fixing" that we often try to do through thinking is not needed. This is often the most difficult thing to learn in meditation. "Do not try to fix anything." Meditation is not a thinking pastime; it is a stilling of the activity of mind so that it can be more easily watched.

With this stillness, we can begin to observe the mind with mindfulness. "Mindfulness" is observation of the mind. It is the mind's ability to skillfully contemplate itself through recollection, reflection, and self-awareness; it is an essential part of the development of true wisdom. This is not the same as the memory-based thinking that one uses for studying before an exam but is an intuitive wisdom which is experienced rather than thought. With appropriate concentration and mindfulness, we become the observer of the activity of the mind.

To be present with what is going on within the mind at every moment, while being in or out of meditation, is the ideal situation for every person. This is what leads to a true understanding of the mind.

Basic instructions for meditation

Meditation is generally done with the eyes closed, the chin slightly lifted, and the spine erect but relaxed. One should start their practice with the feeling of being comfortable.

In a place where you can be alone, or with like minded people, and where there are few distractions, bring yourself to a comfortable seated posture. You can sit on the floor with the legs crossed upon a cushion or folded blanket. Do not lean against a wall, but learn to keep the posture upright and steady. There are those who will have difficulties and discomfort sitting on the floor. If this is the situation, you should simply sit in a straight-back chair with both feet flat on the floor. It is best to be comfortable and meditate for shorter periods of time rather than to fight with discomfort. Whatever posture you are using, whether on the floor or in a chair, one should always attempt to keep the back relaxed but fairly straight. This will help with the level of energy that flows up and down the body.

When practicing meditation, we must have an object to rest our concentration upon. The practices within this book will be using the breath as the object of meditation. The breath will be explained in great detail, both as the primary and secondary object of meditation. As previously mentioned, the breath will, at times, be the main area of concentration, and at other times, it will be present but in the background.

The Buddha and mindfulness of breathing

The Buddha lived in India approximately 2600 years ago. He left the comforts of a wealthy family life in his earlier years, in order to find freedom from the suffering of Birth, Aging, Sickness, and Death that every human goes through, not only in one lifetime but through many lifetimes as one is reborn from life to life. This was the common belief at that time, as well as today, for many spiritual traditions.

The Buddha tried different spiritual practices involving different forms of meditation. He eventually had a profound breakthrough, while in deep meditation and became fully enlightened through his practice. As a result of his enlightenment, the Buddha taught the Dhamma: the true nature of reality. He did so for the remainder of his life. His teachings grew into what we call today, Buddhism.

At one time, toward the end of a three-month long meditation retreat, the Buddha looked out onto the large group of meditation practitioners. These meditation practitioners were his followers and had been meditating with him for the entire retreat. The

Buddha saw the well-learned monks teaching large and small groups of meditators who were studying and practicing meditation. He saw how everyone was greatly benefiting by the meditation retreat and the meditation teachings that were being given. He looked out on the calm and silent gathering and was very happy. The Buddha was so pleased that he decided to stay in this place for one more month to continue to practice meditation.

It was then that the Buddha gave the instructions on Mindfulness of Breathing, namely, *"The Anapanasati"*. He addressed the practitioners, explaining the Anapanasati by breaking the practice into four groups. Within each group are four areas of practice, making the entire practice consist of a total of sixteen areas.

The sixteen areas of the Anapanasati

The following chart provides an overall look at the sixteen areas, or steps, of this practice. We will progress through each of these areas within this book. Each area will start with the Sutta as spoken by the Buddha. This is followed by a thorough explanation, or commentary, of each area. Every other area is followed with a written out, guided meditation. This is to help further your understanding of the specific meditation practice.

The purpose of the guided meditations is to enable the meditator to better understand the object of the meditation, as well as how to use the specific meditation object in your practice. The *guiding* element of this type of meditation practice is not necessarily for one to rely on the specific words, but the idea and direction to which the words point.

When using guided meditations, the words are often recited or spoken out load by someone, or played from a recording. It is suggested that one not rely on guided meditations, but use them as a tool for learning. Guided meditations should be used to indicate what direction the specific meditation is meant to take the meditator. Each of these practices should be memorized and internalized in order to be of the utmost benefit. The following chart is meant to be an aid in this process and could be copied and kept near ones meditation area for reference.

Anapanasati Sutta

Body	• Long Breath • Short Breath • Experiencing the Breath and Body • Calming the Body
Feelings	• Experiencing Rapture • Experiencing Pleasure • Experiencing all Feelings • Calming all Feelings
Mind state	• Experiencing the Mind • Gladdening the Mind • Concentrating the Mind • Liberating the Mind
Dhammas	• Contemplating Impermanence • Contemplating Fading away • Contemplating Cessation • Contemplating Relinquishment

Mindfulness Of Body

We must always begin our meditation by placing our awareness on the body. This is a natural process since we must first get the body to the place of meditation. We then make the body comfortable and experience it settling into its meditation posture. Then, we can bring our attention to another aspect of the body: the breathing body; the breath.

Throughout our day, the breath is often taken for granted. Normally, we pay very little attention to the breath unless we have a lack of healthy oxygen or find it uncomfortable to breathe in some way. In truth, the fact that we pay so little attention to it, is the reason it makes a wonderful meditation object; it is subtle. In observing the breath while in meditation, we will likely find that it is much more interesting and much more useful than previously realized.

The breath is with us every moment of our lives, which also makes it an ideal object to observe when meditating. The breath acts as an anchor for us to rest our attention on and to help keep the mind from wandering. The breath is like a flagpole to hang onto in a windstorm. In other words, it is our place to come back to when we notice our attention has wandered off.

Mindfulness of breathing is a practice that leads to stability of mind through concentration. The stability of mind comes as a direct result of the slowing of thoughts. The ability to remain focused on the breath acts as an antidote to mental distraction and unnecessary mental activity.

We start our meditation practice with a very subtle and wonderful object to focus our attention on, the breath.

Note:

Below each of the headings of each area, #1 through #16, you will find the instructions as given by the Buddha in the discourse "The Anapanasati Sutta". After every other explanation of each area of the Sutta, there will be a meditation practice. There are eight meditations in all.

Mindfulness of Body, #1 The Long Breath

"While breathing in long, he fully comprehends, 'I breathe in long.' While breathing out long, he fully comprehends, 'I breathe out long'".
The Buddha

The long breath can be explained as being called "the long breath" because of the observation of one of the aspects of the breath. When we breathe, the breath enters and then leaves the body. As the breath enters this is the inhalation. As it leaves the body, this is the exhalation.

What the Buddha called "the long breath" is not a breath made long by breathing more air into the lungs. Nor is it made by breathing slower and longer than normal. It is called the long breath because of how we are observing the breath.

If we where to imagine our breathing in an upward and downward motion, the inhalation being an upward movement and the exhalation being a downward movement, we might also imagine them being similar to the two sides of a wave. The lines in the following diagram resemble this. The point that we are full of air, as we breathe air into the body, is the top of the inhalation. As we exhale the air that is in the body, this is the exhalation.

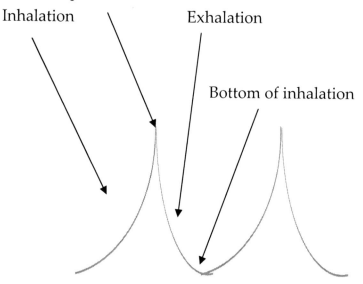

The top of the inhalation

Inhalation

Exhalation

Bottom of inhalation

When we do breath meditation, in order to refine our area of concentration, the emphasis of our attention is either placed on the top of the inhalation or on the bottom. When the attention is on the bottom of the exhalation, this is the long breath. With the attention on the bottom of the breath, the breath naturally becomes long.

The long breath can be related to the very last breath that we will take in this life. The last thing we will do in this life is a *long* exhalation of the breath.

The long breath is relaxing and calming. When used properly, it can remedy restlessness and worry and still the mental activity that is generally noticed during meditation, particularly in the early stages of the practice.

One method that helps to provide a clear understanding of this practice and the calming effect that it provides is counting the breath. By placing the count of the breath at bottom of the inhalation, the breath will feel as if it is lengthening without being consciously manipulated. When counting the long breaths, we place the count exactly at the bottom of the exhalation just before we start the inhalation.

There is a point where there is a complete stillness of the breath. It is directly at this point where we place the number or the count. Counting the breaths should be done easily and in rhythm with the breath but not in a mechanical or habitual way. It takes focus and concentration to keep ones full attention on where the count is placed. This is why it can be such a calming addition to the practice of breath meditation.

Counting the breathes

Counting the number of breaths is an optional part of a meditation practice. Many will begin their practice counting and then find that it is no longer necessary. Others may use counting throughout their entire practice, and still others may occasionally consider using it only when excessive mental activity is noticed.

Counting is simply an additional aspect of the practice that gives the meditator a little more to do, at least until the mind slows down from its habitual fast pace. Many count the number of breaths up to 10, and then either start over or count backwards from 10 to 1. There are many who count up 21, this being the average number of breaths one breathes in a two-minute period. The advantage to counting in this manner is that if a person wanted to count their breath for the first ten minutes of their meditation practice they would count up to 21 breaths, five times. This equals ten minutes of counting the breath. Many use a 21-bead wrist mala, or bracelet, as an aid in this practice.

Again, counting is optional and something that everyone should experiment with since it can provide an excellent and fast way to get beyond what some refer to as the "monkey mind." The monkey is a reference to the untrained mind that continually jumps from thought to thought like the monkey that continually jumps from limb to limb. Simply put, counting the breaths helps to gather up the mental activity and hold it in one area.

Mindfulness of Body, #2 The Short Breath

"While breathing in short, he fully comprehends, 'I breathe in short.' While breathing out short, he fully comprehends, 'I breathe out short.'"
The Buddha

The short breath is easily understood, if one has already practiced the long breath, since it is its opposite. We could refer to the short breath as the "other side of the wave" or the up and down motion of the cycle of breathing. Our emphasis when working with the short breath is at the top of the inhalation. If we were to count the number of breathes we would place the emphasis of the count at the very top of the inhalation, after the breath enters the body.

The short breath is the energizing breath and can be used to wake up and give energy to the body and bring alertness to the mind and mental activity. With fatigue and drowsiness being a very common problem with many meditators, both advanced and beginners, the long breath, as a source of energy, can be a most welcome and useful tool in the meditation practice.

When working with the long breath for a period of time and then moving into the short breath, you should notice a profound shift in your level of energy. This is brought about by the placement of your awareness alone, and not by a change in the breath.

Your breath may subtly change, and we should allow it to do so although that is not the goal of this meditation. Your job is to notice the changes in the body as you change the placement of your awareness.

Knowing how to use the long and short breaths to manipulate your energy level is a very useful thing to know in and out of meditation. If you feel tired, try revitalizing your energy by using the short breath. If you are feeling any anxiety or hyperactivity, try calming this by using the long breath.

Meditation-Comprehending the long and short breaths

* Ellipses (. . .) are used in all of the meditations through-out this book. These are used to represent moments of stillness. Each ellipse represents one full in-and-out breath. Three ellipses equal an approximate pause of twenty seconds.

In a quiet place with few distractions, bring yourself to a comfortable, seated posture while keeping the back straight. If sitting in a chair, refrain from lean-ing against the back. If sitting with crossed legs upon a cushion on the floor, elevate the body by keeping the knees low and the seat high. This will help keep the back straight and comfortable. The eyes can be closed or slightly opened. The chin is slightly lifted.

Once the body is relaxed, bring your attention to the breath. Think in terms of the body breathing on its own. There is no intentional manipulation of the breath. Our primary activity will be to experience the natural breath in a way that we have never done before. We begin by simply noticing the breath when we are drawing air into the body. . .

Now, take notice of the breath as it leaves the body on each exhalation. . .

Take a few moments, and notice the inhalation; the air coming into the body. . .

Continue breathing normally, but while exhaling the breath, bring your attention to and find the pause, or gap, that can be found at the end of the exhalation. . .

This pause can be found immediately before you breathe in. . .

Do this again, after you exhale. Notice the gap before you inhale; do not make it any longer or shorter. Just notice it. . .

Breathe in and exhale noticing the gap, and breathe in again. . .

Do this on your own for awhile; exhale; notice the gap, and breathe in. . .

This noticing of the gap after the exhalation is the factor that determines the long breath; we breathe out (there is a gap), and then we breathe in. . .

Keep your awareness on the gap after the exhalation of the breath. . .

Stay with the gap as we inhale and exhale. . .

Here, we are keeping our awareness on the gap; we are not following the breath as it flows in and out or noticing the air coming into and leaving the body. We are not noticing anything except the gap. . .

See if you can experience this: breathing in, and then breathing out while keeping your attention on the gap throughout the complete inhalation and exhalation. . .

Now, notice how this way of focusing on the breath affects you. . .

Is this way of focusing on the breath calming and relaxing?. . .

The long breath is used to still the mind of its many thoughts and to relax the body. Simply place your

attention on the bottom of the exhalation, notice the gap, and breathe...

This is the long breath...

Now, if you are familiar with the long breath. We can move on to the short breath; the second step in the *Anapanasati* ...

[The short breath]

The short breath is used to bring energy into the body. Again, we are not manipulating the breath but are centering our focus on an aspect of the breath. Just as we did with the long breath, we work with the gap. The short breath is the opposite of the long breath. The breathing is the same, but our point of focus is the opposite.

As we inhale, notice how we meet with the gap at the top of the inhalation...

It is there each time we breathe inward...

Immediately after landing on the gap, we exhale...

We meet the gap at the top of our inhalation, our point of focus, and then we exhale. . .

Breathe though it; continue breathing . . .

Now, see if you can rest your attention on that gap after the inhalation; it should feel energizing...

It should feel like a completely different way of breathing although it is simply breathing...

Breathing in, feel the gap; breathing out. . .

Breathing in, keep your attention on the gap; breathing out. . .

Keep your focus on the gap while continuing to breathe through it. . .

Breathing in and out. . .

Do this on your own, and notice how it creates energy and alertness in mind and body. . .

Breathing in and breathing out. . .

Continue practicing for as long as time permits. . .

As you get comfortable with long and short breath meditations, you can alternate between them, incorporating relaxation and energy as you desire. Try doing one of them five or ten minutes and then the other, alternating between them.

Mindfulness of Body, #3 Experiencing the Breath and Body

"He trains himself, 'Thoroughly experiencing the breath and body, I shall breathe in.' He trains himself, 'Thoroughly experiencing the breath and body, I shall breathe out.'"

The Buddha

In this area of the Anapanasati, the above instructions change from comprehending the breath and the breathing body, to training (e.g. "He trains himself"). We are now training our ability to use the breath as our primary or secondary object of meditation rather than simply a focal point.

For many people, it is easy to imagine the breath moving in a vertical manner up and down the body. [See the diagram below] It may be helpful to visualize the breath traveling through the core of the body from the tip of the nose to the navel and back again, without pause, in a flowing motion.

This way of breathing can allow our focus and awareness to settle into an area of the body in a natural or controlled way. The area of focus will have a tendency to affect the calming and energizing of the body and can be used for whichever is needed or desired at any given time.

We should continue to think of our breathing as the "long breath" being the relaxing exhalation and the "short breath" being the energizing inhalation. These two will, now, simply be looked at as a whole. In this step, "Experiencing the breath and body", we are now looking at the in-and-out breath as a complete cycle of breathing. The breath is continually coming in and going out, a cycle, just like the days and nights, and the seasons and years.

When we breathe in, the air we take in can be looked at the same as if we are bringing energy into the body, which we are. When we breathe out and expel carbon dioxide, we can look at this as a moment of relaxation. Breathing in, energizes. Breathing out, relaxes.

This method of looking at what we would typically think of as our normal cycle of breathing provides several advantages. First, it is an excellent method for stabilizing our meditation posture; as we breathe in, we energize the body. This can be felt as a straightening of the spine, a slight, upward tilt of the chin, and a general lifting of the body. Second, the exhalations help to decrease stress in the muscles of the body; as we breathe out, we soften the body tissue.

The result of this way of practice is that one can sit comfortably for long periods of time while staying alert, yet relaxed. Perhaps the greatest advantage is that it becomes easy to notice when our concentration is no longer on the breath. If we feel sluggish, drowsy and uncomfortable or if the body is tense and it feels like we are struggling to hold on to a decent posture, these are signs that we are not focusing on the practice.

Mindfulness of Body, #4 Calming the Body

"He trains himself, 'Calming the body, I shall breathe in.' He trains himself, 'Calming the body, I shall breathe out.'"
The Buddha

This step of the sutta points to the calming of the body as a practice in and of itself. We are to take the calming effect of the exhalation of the breath and use this to its fullest extent. This will provide a deeper understanding.

To understand the calming of the body, is to thoroughly investigate how the body is functioning in relation to itself. Namely, how we hold particular postures and tense particular muscles when in stressful situations and how this can easily turn into habitual patterns that can cause skeletal problems, compounded stress and disease in the present and future.

In calming of the body, we use a common technique called scanning. To scan, means to examine or investigate the body in a step-by-step sweeping motion. This is often done by relaxing one section of the body at a time. When doing this practice, we start at the top of the body and work our way down.

The process, explained here, is done in a 21-step sequence. It is often done while using the breath in conjunction. To further explain: if we are counting the breath, we would count one breath as well as one area of the body, on each count. With 21 areas of the body (one area with each count of the breath) we would use 21 breaths to scan the entire body.

In the following diagram, the individual areas of the body are shown. They must be memorized in order to get the best calming effect from this meditation. If your visualization is good, you can use it to visualize each part of the body and think in terms of five parts in each group. The groups are as follows:

A). The head.
1. Forehead,
2. Eyes and ears,
3. Cheeks,
4. Jaw,
5. Tongue,

B). The neck and down the arms into the hands.
6. Neck,
7. Shoulders,
8. Biceps,

9. Forearms,

10. Hands,

C). The torso.

11. Upper back,

12. Chest,

13. Middle back and diaphragm,

14. Lower back,

15. Abdomen,

D). The hips and legs.

16. Hips,

17. Thighs,

18. Knees,

19. Shins and calves,

20. Feet

Four groups, twenty areas in all, with the twenty-first count being the full body.

Calming the body with the breath (body scan)

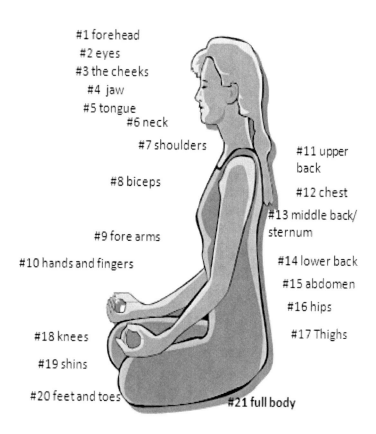

#1 forehead
#2 eyes
#3 the cheeks
#4 jaw
#5 tongue
#6 neck
#7 shoulders
#8 biceps
#9 fore arms
#10 hands and fingers
#11 upper back
#12 chest
#13 middle back/ sternum
#14 lower back
#15 abdomen
#16 hips
#17 Thighs
#18 knees
#19 shins
#20 feet and toes
#21 full body

To practice this method of scanning, it is best to memorize the twenty areas of the body. Then, begin at the top of the body, at the head, and relax each area with an exhalation of the breath. If counting the breaths, place a number at each area of the body, with each exhalation of the breath. You will be doing this twenty times. The final count (21) will be a quick, complete, all-body scan.

Meditation-Experiencing and calming the breath and body

Sit comfortably and bring your attention to the breath. . .

Feel the sensation of the breath at the top of the inhalation in the same way you did in step #1, "the short breath". . .

Alternately, feel the sensation of the breath at the bottom of the exhalation as you did in step #2, "the long breath". . .

Find these two areas of the cycle of breathing, the gaps of the short breath and the long breath. . .

As you inhale, use this breath to bring energy into the body helping to gently improve and maintain a nice meditation posture. . .

Every time you take an "in breath", feel strength and energy come into the body. . .

Feel the body respond with a stabilizing of the posture. . .

Keep the emphasis of the breath at the gap on the top of the inhalation. . .

Feel the subtle adjustments made in the straightening of the back, lifting of the chin, and the opening of the chest. . .

[Calming the body]

Exhale; feel the relaxing effect of the breath as it leaves the body. . .

Place the emphasis of this breath at the gap at the bottom of the exhalation. . .

At the bottom of each exhalation, relax more deeply, just as we did with the long breath. . .

Place the emphasis of your relaxation on each area of the body as you exhale.
Beginning at the top of the body, the head, on an exhalation, relax the forehead.

Inhale, stabilizing your posture.
Exhale, relaxing the eyes.
Inhale.
Exhale, relaxing the cheeks.
Inhale; feel the air as energy.
Exhale, relaxing the jaw.
Inhale.
Exhale, relaxing the tongue.
Inhale; straighten the back.
Exhale, relaxing the neck.
Inhale.
Exhale, relaxing the shoulders.
Inhale.
Exhale, relaxing the biceps.
Inhale.
Exhale, relaxing the forearms.
Inhale.
Exhale; relax the hands and fingers.
Inhale.
Exhale; relax the upper back.
Inhale.
Exhale, relaxing the upper chest.
Inhale.
Exhale, relaxing the middle back and diaphragm.
Inhale.

Exhale, relaxing the lower back.

Inhale.

Exhale, relaxing the abdomen.

Inhale.

Exhale, relaxing the hips.

Inhale.

Exhale; relax the thighs.

Inhale.

Exhale, relaxing the knees.

Inhale.

Exhale, relaxing the shins.

Inhale.

Exhale, relaxing the feet.

Inhale.

Exhale, with a complete body sweep.

Inhale.

Use the in-and-out breath as a whole, as a complete cycle of breathing. . .

Stabilize and energize the body with each inhalation. . .

Use the exhalation to relax and calm. . .

Notice how it feels to have this calm, silent power within. . .

Practice for as long as time allows. . . .

Mindfulness of Feelings

Typically, the sense organs of the body are thought of as the eyes, ears, nose, mouth and skin. Sense objects are anything that is seen, heard, smelled, tasted or felt. In Buddhism, thoughts are considered a sixth sense. When a sense organ comes into contact with a sense object, including thought, there is a corresponding feeling that is created at that moment of contact. These feelings are generally very brief and quickly change, but noticing and working with them is an invaluable part of our practice of mindfulness.

Feelings, in Buddhist terminology, are much different than the western term which is more closely related to emotions and has a much broader meaning. It is often easier to think of the feelings that we refer to in Buddhist terms as sensations. The western term *emotions* is more closely linked to mind states, the topic in the following section, "Mindfulness of Mind States".

The feelings that we are discussing here can be easily placed into one of three areas: pleasant, unpleasant and neutral. When we think of something and use the mind to reflect back in time, we can re-call a happy experience. This produces a pleasant feeling. We can do the opposite as well; we can use the mind to imagine possible negative future events, causing restlessness and worry. The result is our ex-periencing of unpleasant feelings due to thought connecting with the perception of our imagined negative future or the perceived negative memory of the past.

Feelings are arising at every moment. As we be-come aware of the activity of our feelings, we can use this to our advantage. To control our feelings is to control our life. We can become the one in charge and no longer follow the commands of feeling if we choose not to. It is through awareness and under-standing of these feelings that this can happen.

To understand our feelings is to understand that we spend most of our time looking and moving to-ward the things in life that we believe will bring us lasting happiness. Alternatively, we spend the other portion of our time moving away from the unplea-sant things in life.

There is much joy to be found in this life. To be aware and in control of what we are doing in order to find and have joy is the key to having true happi-ness. This happiness does not rely on material ob-jects but comes from within. The type of happiness that the sages teach us to be aware of and to incorporate into our lives is found through the practice of meditation and ultimately through the understanding of the mind.

By discovering our inner joy and happiness, we learn to work with the unpleasant things in life through acceptance. To accept is to remove the negativity from the things we find unpleasant and learn to see them as a necessary part of life and our growth. We must have unpleasant and even painful experiences in order to better understand the pleasant ones. This is similar to the way in which we cannot fully comprehend what heat is without knowing of its opposite cold.

The following meditations work with feelings. We begin with the pleasant but unstable feeling of rapture and then on to joy and pleasure. These pleasant and happy feelings are a natural result of concentration and mindfulness. They are the natural byproduct of a consistent practice in meditation.

We will then work with the ability to notice the continual movement of the feelings as they arise, by being sensitive to all of them. Ultimately, through noticing, this will bring an awareness that allows us to work with the calming of the feelings by stopping the habitual running toward pleasant and away from unpleasant feelings.

The meditation practices in this area are still centered on the use of the breath. Those that pertain to this area should be considered an extension of the previous breath meditation practices. Within this area we are now bringing a portion of our awareness to the recognition of feelings as they arise. We will be focusing our attention on the breath, while at the same time becoming acquainted with feelings.

Mindfulness of Feelings, #5 Experiencing Rapture (Piti)

"He trains himself, 'Thoroughly experiencing rapture (piti), I shall breathe in.' He trains himself, 'Thoroughly experiencing rapture (piti), I shall breath out.'"
The Buddha,

Piti is a Pali word that describes rapture. This is a natural state that arises when there is a feeling such as accomplishment. It is an exciting and happy, stimulating feeling that is filled with joy and satisfaction. It very much resembles a feeling of success that is optimistically humble. It is often a factor in being motivated to do something. It is the opposite of the feeling that one has when depressed, which is often found in conjunction with sadness and a lack of enthusiasm for life.

Rapture can start out as being very subtle and difficult to notice, and then it can take off and become the only thing noticed. When piti arises and becomes strong in meditation, it can actually be a disturbance to our practice. This is because of the distractions that the excited mental activity of piti causes. When looked at with mindfulness, however, we will see that this is not always a bad situation. We will be able to see rapture as a feeling, and experience it for what it is.

Piti can be experienced both through concentration and through insight. To understand what it is, it might be helpful get a feel for it by doing the following: Think of a time when you felt very happy and successful. Perhaps there was a time when you landed that great job or when you scored very high on a test or won a contest. Piti can be related to that "yes" feeling you get when these situations arise. Once you notice piti, the identification and the engaged awareness is what allows it to build through the practice of insight. It is through the contemplation aspect of insight that piti is experienced, or we could say revisited.

The second method of experiencing piti is through concentration itself. When the mind becomes deeply concentrated, without wavering or leaving the object of concentration, it temporarily sets aside all negativity and worry. The result is similar to when we shift the gears of a car into neutral. The mind is not in a pleasant or unpleasant place. In other words, the mind is not affected by worldly sensations. Feelings are not arising. When in this place of neutrality, between pleasant and unpleasant, we are experiencing our true nature.

Our true nature is peace and joy, a mental place where there are no worries or mind-made problems. Through concentration, we can place ourselves in a state where everything is perfect. It is important to remember that, although a perfect place, this state of deep concentration is temporary. We can learn to access rapture or piti through a consistent practice in meditation. Once experienced, it can point us to the knowing that true liberation is from suffering possible, and it is available here and now through skillful concentration.

When we reflect on this experience that we had as a result of concentration, what arises is joy and rapture. This reflection can be accomplished within the same meditation period that the deep concentration was experienced, or at a later time. It is an actual recall of the experience of being free from the "push and pull" of pleasant and unpleasant feelings. It is a mental freedom which is based on the ability of the mind to let go.

With regard to your daily meditation practice; While progressing through each of these steps of the *Anapanasati*, one should always start with step one, until completely familiar with each area of practice. This will strengthen your understanding of the subtleness and profundity of each area of this practice.

With practice, you will likely find that you may choose to allocate varying amounts of time to some preferred steps. This is fine, however, always progress sequentially through the steps.

Mindfulness of Feelings, #6 Experiencing Pleasure (Sukha)

"He trains himself, 'Thoroughly experiencing sukha, I shall breathe in.' He trains himself, 'Thoroughly experiencing sukha, I shall breathe out.'"
The Buddha

In the last step, we mentioned that rapture is an exciting and happy feeling and is experienced through concentration as well as insight. In this step we will notice the pleasure of a tranquil, peaceful joy that is soothing and more subtle than rapture. It is what follows the activated quality of rapture. It too comes from the result of concentration and insight meditation practices. *Sukha* is a Pali word meaning joyful or pleasant. Unlike rapture it is more sustaining and easier to sit with in a peaceful way because it does not contain any form of restlessness. It is soothing and calming.

When meditating with the breath, the breath becomes very pleasant and calm, producing a deep stillness in the body and mind. It is sometimes referred to as the beautiful breath because of the pleasing quality it has. Sukha is the warm, comfortable, steady joy that allows one to meditate for long periods of time. Often, one will not wish to stop their meditation but remain still and peaceful. This is a good indication that the meditation practice is working and that sukha is present.

Because of its nature, sukha can stay with us for long periods of time. It can even remain with us long after our formal meditation practice and many claim that it can literally change the way we see the world. Sukha carries with it the strong feeling that everything is okay just as it is. It is a wonderful feeling that is a natural by-product of a correct meditation practice as well as correct living.

Meditation-Experiencing rapture and pleasure

Bring yourself to a comfortable posture. . .

Relax the eyes; feel the body as it settles into its posture, keeping the back straight and the chin up. .

Bring your awareness to the present thoughts that you are now having. . .

As you draw your attention to these thoughts, think in terms of only lightly touching them with awareness. . .

Experience the thoughts, in a way that you are not taking them seriously, just looking at them. . .

Experience the thoughts knowing that you will be leaving them behind completely as you do these practices. . .

See all thoughts and mental activity as something that can be placed on hold and seen through. . .

Silently tell yourself that all planning, all mental and physical activity, will be ignored while you do this meditation. . .

Slowly bring your attention to the breath. . .

As you notice the breath, see the mental energy become less and less . . .

Notice what your attention is placed upon. . .

Take a few moments and feel the beginning, middle, and end of each in-and-out breath. . .

Now, refine your breath awareness to one specific area. Either bring your attention to the top of the inhalation, or the bottom of the exhalation. . .

Find the gap...

This place, this gap; make it your only point of awareness. . .

It is your only concern; nothing is more important at this time. . .

How does it feel? . . .

[Pleasure (sukha)]

With the body comfortable and with the eyes relaxed, reflect on the experience of the concentrated mind. . .

Feel the joy of having freedom from the "push and pull" of feelings. . .

Imagine the pure, clear mind, the mind unburdened by feelings and thought. . .

A mind that is uncluttered and completely free of obstruction. . .

Experience the naturally arising joy and happiness that comes from this freedom. . .

Like being freed from a lifetime of mental imprisonment. . .

Understand that this is your true nature. . .

Experience the mind that does not have to hold on to thoughts, feelings, or emotions. . .

The concentrated, unburdened, joyful mind. . .

Continue in silence for as long as time permits. . .

Mindfulness of Feelings, #7 Experiencing All Feelings

"He trains himself, 'Being sensitive to all feelings, I shall breathe in.' He trains himself, 'Being sensitive to all feelings, I shall breathe out.'"
The Buddha

In the same way that we noticed in step 1 and 2 how the breath can condition and influence the body to be calmer or to be more energized, we will now take the opportunity to notice how feelings influence the mind in much the same way.

It is important to realize that every time our senses come into contact with a sense object, there is an associated feeling that arises. Feelings are appearing all of the time, at every moment of our daily activities. That is why it is vital that we learn to identify and understand our feelings, so that we no longer become slaves to them. When we encounter something in our life that we find pleasant, we are pulled toward it by our feelings. In the same way, when we encounter something that we find unpleasant, there is a pushing away. The alternative to this constant pulling and pushing that seems to be directed by our feelings is found in the understanding, watching and ultimately the control of this process.

In this step, experiencing all feelings, we are working with the mindfulness of the development and changing aspect of feelings. There are several exercises that can help with this meditation.

When beginning your meditation, take special notice of the general feeling you are experiencing with the breath at that very moment. Ask, "Does the breath feel pleasant, unpleasant or neutral?" This line of questioning places your awareness directly on the feeling you are experiencing with the object; the breath. The breath is mostly a touch type of feeling. After staying with this for a while ask yourself, "How does my body feel in terms of the other touch sensations?" "What is the feeling associated with the pressure from sitting and any other bodily discomforts, or bodily pleasures."

Expand this practice further by using smells and sounds. Notice if there are any pleasant or unpleasant feelings associated with the sounds and smells you are currently experiencing. Next, notice the feelings associated with the mind, in terms of thoughts, and how the uncontrolled thoughts of the past and future stir up feelings.

When we do this practice, our awareness is such that we are dividing our attention between the breath and the feeling that we are experiencing at this moment. It is important to remember that we are merely noticing the presence of the feelings and not trying to change or judge them. The awareness alone is enough to change things in a favorable way. We are not trying to take control with forced manipulation. We are taking control through intelligent awareness.

Mindfulness of Feelings, #8 Calming All Feelings

"He trains himself, 'Calming all feelings, I shall breathe in.' He trains himself, 'Calming all feelings, I shall breathe out.'"
The Buddha

In step #8, our work with feelings goes beyond our association with the feelings and into the calming of them. To calm our feelings is to further understand them and know them for what they are and how they can lead to craving.

When a sense experience arises such as seeing hearing, tasting, smelling, touching and cognizing (or thought) we must learn to observe this experience as just being sight, sound, taste, odor, touch and thinking. Whenever we notice these feelings, we should simply notice whether they are pleasant, unpleasant or neutral.

The only way that feelings can take the form of craving, which is what we must avoid, is when we take a personal interest in the experience. Craving is like a lingering residue left behind from a short-lived, pleasant experience. It is like a mental magnet that is continually pulling us toward something that we previously found to be pleasant. The pull can be so strong that even while we are experiencing the craved thing, we could be thinking of and building on the craving. We could be thinking of our next meal while we are eating. Cravings easily can turn into addictions.

At its deepest level, in regard to feelings, if we think that "I" like this or "I" don't like that or think in terms of "I" want to make that "mine", we are attempting to make the sense object something other than what it is by applying ownership to it. In applying ownership to it, we are believing that the world should be other than what it is.

We must learn to be simply an observer of our feelings and know that we do not have to always react to them. The only thing we need to do is be present with what is arising in each present moment. This is the calming of feelings.

There is a second group of feelings. Up until now we have been dealing with "worldly feelings", these being the feelings that are brought about by sense objects, the worldly things that we see, hear, smell, taste, touch and think about. This second kind of feelings is called "unworldly feelings". These are the kind of feelings that the Buddha said were the

correct kind of feelings to enjoy and learn to cultivate. These unworldly feelings are the feelings we
are actually working with and trying to better understand in meditation. When concentrated, we can
experience these as being pleasant feelings that are
not related to people, places or things. Unworldly
feelings are brought about by high levels of serenity
and from "going within".

Unworldly feelings are those feelings that we
have that are related to our progress in meditation
or the spiritual path. Some see them as more of a
psychological feeling as opposed to a physiological
one.

A very simple example might be the feeling one
has when they have finished a good meditation ses-
sion; it is the joyful result from that practice. It is also the joy that is a result from deep concentration.

These unworldly feelings are the feelings we
should learn to recognize because they are beneficial
for us and provide a virtuous joy. They can also be
the fuel that propels us to continue and deepen our
meditation practice.

Meditation-Experiencing and calming all feelings

In a comfortable posture, calm the body and relax the eyes closed. . .

Allow yourself to become sensitive to everything in and around you. . .

What are you hearing?. . . Is there an associated feeling? . . .

What are you visualizing? . . . Is there a feeling arising from this experience?. . .

What are you tasting or smelling? . . . Is there a feeling that follows?. . .

What are you feeling in the body? . . . Is there pleasantness or unpleasantness associated with the body at this time?. . .

What thoughts are arising at this time? . . . Can they be simply watched without reaction? . . .

Be the one who experiences without reacting to all worldly activity as it is now happening. . .

Imagine, at this moment, that you are simply the one who investigates the feelings that are arising...

You are the watcher...

Think of a craving that you may have recently experienced or are possibly currently experiencing . . .

Can you see where that craving has lead you? . .

Can you imagine being able to see all craving without the need to react? . .

How would that change your life? . .

Imagine all of the feelings you encounter on a daily basis. . . Now imagine being able to easily, and effortlessly let go of them all. . .

Wipe clean the residue of craving and hanging onto feelings, any feelings. . .

See the pleasant feelings, the unpleasant feelings, and the neutral feelings...

See them for what they are...

Understand your inner, unworldly experiences and feelings...

Know that the unworldly feelings that lay within are the feelings that are true and are to be cultivated.

Continue for as long as time permits. . . . .

Mindfulness of Mind States

Mind states are the result of sensations, perceptions, and the many thoughts that we have on a regular basis. Just as the feelings that we previously looked at are continually present, so are the mind states. They are rising and falling away within the mind continuously, moment by moment. We are experiencing a particular mind state or a combination of several of them at this moment. A state is a condition; a mind state is a particular condition of the mind that we can experience at any given time.

There are many different types of mind states and many different degrees. They may be felt as a state of being happy, sad, focused, confused, angry, calm, fearful, ashamed, or confident. Just about any word that we typically use to describe our mental attitude or emotion at a particular moment can be considered a mind state. There are beneficial or positive mind states as well as negative ones.

Typically, we simply just experience the mind states and not consider watching or attempting to recognize them. Although, mind states can be watched and this is the task of mindfulness: to clearly recognize the state of mind that underlies a particular activity or thought.

The primary three negative mind states that we continually come across when developing our ability to understand and recognize the mind states are: *Greed, Aversion and Delusion*. Upon investigation and contemplation, it will be discovered that these three are the main roots to all unhealthy mental events.

Greed is anything that we have a tendency to move toward, such as something we crave or desire. *Aversion* is a "pushing away" and can take the form of anger, hatred or disliking in any form. *Delusion* is a mental confusion. This arises when the mind is lacking sufficient information to settle on a conclusion about something, like the feeling one has when lost. The mind seems to spin without direction, not knowing where to land. It can also be expressed as a type of ignorance. This is seen when we worry about something that has not yet happened, or spend time in restlessness, not sure of what action we should take toward a subject.

It is very worthwhile to mention that the contemplation of the mind states does not involve any active measures to oppose these unwholesome states of mind. We are to simply remain aware, and clearly recognize the states without any kind of judgment. We should not have any regard toward something being "right" or "wrong" or impose any type of mental commentary, since this would only result in the mind creating, or attaching, a personal story to the mind state.

We have a strong tendency to create situations for ourselves that require a decision to be made. This is where our mind chatter comes from, as well as our trying to mentally fix things by thinking our way out of a situation. Anytime we have an agenda, whether it is during our meditation or not, we can find ourselves being motivated by thought, and even more so, thinking. In reality, the mind mostly gets in the way of our practice, so while we are trying to be mindful and practicing meditation, this is not the time for agendas or problem fixing. This would be similar to an overly-protective parent not allowing their children to leave the protection of the home and go out and live their lives. We are to allow the mind to move about but with an interested eye, not a restricted one.

We are to experience the minds reactions to life; this is a large part of understanding the mind states and who we are. Our being present to what is arising in each present moment is the only thing that is needed to disarm any unwholesome mind states and to cultivate clarity of mind and mental freedom (liberation) from greed, aversion and delusion.

In the next four steps of our practice, it is worth-while to remind ourselves that all of these steps are to be experienced within the background of the breath. As subtle as it may be, the breath is still very much the foundation of the meditation practice. Without the breath as the foundation of the practice, we would likely be sitting and thinking rather than cultivating concentration and insight. Thinking, of course, is something that can be done outside of our formal meditation practice so there is no need for us to be doing so while attempting to meditate.

Mindfulness of Mind States, #9 Experiencing the Mind

"He trains himself, 'Thoroughly experiencing the mind, I shall breathe in.' He trains himself, 'Thoroughly experiencing the mind, I shall breathe out.'"
The Buddha,

Meditation provides us with the invaluable opportunity for mental discovery. We initiate this by first bringing the mind to a point of stillness through concentration and relaxation. We can then learn from the mind by working with and observing it. The more this is done, the stronger our relationship with the mind. This relationship is based on cooperative understanding and wisdom. This is the basis behind experiencing the mind.

To experience the mind, it is beneficial first to identify the pulling, pushing, and uncertainty of it. Just as if our body were to be pulled and pushed around by another person, negative-mind states do the same to our mental stability. These negative mind states were recently discussed under the umbrella of greed, aversion, and delusion.

The mind states of *greed* are those that are felt as desire. This is felt when the mind comes up with the idea that it would need or like something to help satisfy it. Desire could also be a simple, and often times difficult to notice, wish to change anything to something other than what it already is.

We can experience the "pushing away" effect aversion can have on us in the form of anger, hatred, or fear. It can feel like uncertainty of the future, or of having no control over the given state of affairs, resulting in a pushing away or denial of the situation.

A lack of concentration and wisdom that results in confusion, a lack of clarity, and dullness of mind is *delusion*. This is an uncertainty and anxiety that is the direct result of not having adequate information or of being ignorant about a situation or thing.

We can work with mind states by noticing when they are present or not present. Alternatively, we will learn of their opposites, these being the positive mind states of generosity, loving kindness and wisdom. These beneficial mind states provide a settling and clarity of the mind that is a result from the absence of greed, aversion and delusion.

It was previously mentioned and is important to keep in mind that there is always a mind state present. Those mentioned above are often the easiest to notice and work with. As our practice evolves, we will certainly wish to expand our capacity to notice the many types of mind states that we deal with on a daily basis. This includes the suppressed states such as depression, as well as the exalted states, which are the advanced states that are very possible when doing this practice. Look at all of them with a selfless nature and an awareness that is bare of judgment, where we are simply watching their arising and disappearing. This is where we will be placing our awareness; on the noticing of the mind states as well as remaining on the breath.

The process of understanding the mind can be started by simply asking yourself, "What mind state is being experienced at this moment?" We then watch and, at times, follow the mind state as it changes. If truly mindful, we will know the exact state of mind at each given moment, knowing whether the mind is calm or agitated, lustful or fearful, happy or depressed.

Notice how your awareness of the states tends to change them; generally it will be a sense of softening. Take careful, mindful notice of how this wonderful practice carries through into your daily life, well beyond your formal meditation, which is the ultimate goal.

Mindfulness of Mind States, #10 Gladdening the Mind

"He trains himself, 'Gladdening the mind, I shall breathe in.' He trains himself, 'Gladdening the mind, I shall breathe out.'"
The Buddha

In this step, we allow joyful energy to build into a state of delight or "gladdening". This is accomplished in several ways, through concentration and insight.

This area of the practice differs from the blissful and joyful practices we previously did with feeling. By working with the mind states, we are not only working with the senses or a sense object but are doing a skilled identification, or understanding, of a particular mind state. These mind states are established beyond sensations alone and are brought about by concentration and insight.

Once the joy of deep concentration is experienced, through the meditative practices of training the mind to stay with the breath, we can then use the contemplative practices of insight. The clarity and peacefulness that these experiences produce is a gladdening of the mind. This gladdening, which was originally brought about through concentration, is further reflected upon in meditation and experienced again and again with investigative insight. With a consistent practice, gladdening of the mind can be made stronger and more sustaining.

To summarize, gladdening of the mind can be made into a two-part process; these being concentration and the process of reflection through insight. When reflecting on a gladdening experience that we noticed while in deep concentration, we rest in the awareness of that state in which we are reflecting upon, allowing the gladdening of the mind to build. We are then training the mind to notice and stay with the mind state. This can only occur after first experiencing the state through concentration. The concentrated mind is free from worry and restlessness. It is still and calm. This is the pleased and glad mind.

Notice the overall change in the way you feel when doing this meditation. Do not judge or make any decisions about this gladdening of mind, but simply recall the mind state. Whenever you get the opportunity to practice this meditation, the gladdening of the mind will grow stronger. Whenever the reflection of the gladdening of mind becomes weak in insight, go back to the breath and work in this area of concentration until the mind becomes unmistakably calm and happy.

*Remember to use each of the ellipses as a representation for one complete breath. Don't just read these meditations, memorize the methods and do them.

Meditation–Experiencing and gladdening the mind

In a seated posture, with body and mind relaxed, bring your attention to the breath. . .

Feel both the in and out breaths equally. . .

Notice the mental calming that the practice is providing. . .

Ask, "What mind state am I experiencing at this moment?". . .

Ask, "Can I truly notice and experience this mind state?". . .

Experiencing the mind, is there stability in this state or is it continually moving?. . .

Keeping your attention on the breath, notice if you feel the mind attempting to pull away from the breath and move toward desire. . .

Does the mind have movement, such as pushing out negativity, aversion or fear?. . .

Sit without movement and simply experience the many expressions of the mind. . . . .

[Gladdening the mind]

Take a moment to completely clear the mind of any thoughts. See the mind as a still forest pond, smooth as glass, thoughtless and still. . .

See the mind as a clear cloudless sky. . .

Find the joy that is connected with the still mind and the accompanying lack of thought. . .

Allow yourself to ease into a state of joy; one that is unrelated to the world of form and brought about by concentration and simplicity. . .

Focus and rely on the breath. . .

Notice that the deeper your concentration, the deeper the gladdening of mind. . .

Use this concentration to go within and experience this gladdening of mind. . .

Can you notice a gladdening of mind when you realize that you can be simply the watcher of the mind states? . . .

Silently continue for as long as time permits. . . . .

Mindfulness of Mind States, #11 Concentrating the Mind

"He trains himself, 'Concentrating the mind, I shall breathe in.' He trains himself, 'Concentrating the mind, I shall breathe out,'"
The Buddha

Concentration is an important aspect of all meditation practices, and it is essential for us to have some degree or level of it while we meditate. Without concentration, we will find that we can easily get lost in thought. In many situations, when we apply concentration it can seem as if it is either on or off. Concentration can also feel like it is strong and direct like a laser beam or weak and broad like a dim light bulb gently illuminating a room.

One often overlooked aspect of concentration is that it can be developed and brought under control and directed. Once we have an understanding of concentration it becomes a powerful tool in life. Once we understand its function in our meditation practice, it can change the way we see and feel about everything in our world.

Concentration is a mind state; it plays an important role in everything we do. If we are unable to remain focused on a task we will have trouble completing it in a timely manner without making mistakes along the way. In meditation, concentration plays the vital role of connecting our awareness with our object of meditation. Fortunately for us, the ability to concentrate well can be increased with practice in the same way that exercising a muscle in the body can increase ones physical strength. By using our concentration regularly, it can be improved, which is one of the primary benefits of a regular meditation practice.

It is interesting to note when the mind is very concentrated, and the moment we realize this, it is conceptual. Once the mind becomes conceptual, we then lose our concentration. The thinking that we always thought was such an important thing is actually taking us out of our state of concentration. So it is that our realization of our mind being deeply concentrated comes after the actual experience of this concentration. The mind can only hold onto one object at a time. If our mind is concentrated on an object, there is no way that it can switch from this concentrated state to an analytical thinking state without giving up some of this connection with the object that it is resting upon. This is not a problem if it is understood that we should evaluate the experience after the exercise is finished.

There are three types, or levels, of concentration: momentary, access, and absorption. The first type, momentary, is the common type of concentration that we use when we notice that our concentration is not stable. It is also the type that we use when we are contemplating or placing our attention on something, similar to a controlled type of thinking with an emphasis on staying with the subject.

As an example, we can use a bull's-eye, the center of a target that you try to hit in sports. Imagine not only the bull's-eye but the entire target as your object of meditation. Imagine as well that you continually bring your attention to this target, but there are distractions that hinder this and your concentration is repeatedly, or momentarily, on and off the target. This is momentary concentration.

Access concentration is much more stable. How this happens is when what are called the hindrances, which are the five factors that hinder our ability to concentrate, begin to lose their hold on us. They do not necessarily leave but are very recognizable. These hindrances are: sense desires, ill will, sloth and torpor, restlessness and worry, and doubt. With the dropping away of these hindrances, we can meditate much more easily and for longer periods of time. If using the target and the bull's-eye as examples, we could say that we are on the target.

Absorption is a deeper state of concentration, often called jhana. This state is not easily accessible by the beginning meditator; it only happens when the concentration is made strong after many continuous weeks, months or years of practice. The skilled meditator uses an outlined progression of practice to enter jhana, or deep concentration, at will. All of the hindrances to the practice, mentioned above, fall away and the meditator not only hits the bull's-eye of the target, but with continued practice can do so repeatedly, without effort and can stay there as long as desired. This type of concentration cannot be forced.

The jhanas consist of five factors that allow the veils of the distracted "you" to be pulled away. There is nothing gained or added but more of a revealing of your true nature. You do not gain concentration but lose the things that do not allow this type of concentration to be present. There are five jhana factors, and each of these neutralizes one of the five hindrances. Again, the hindrances are mental states that disrupt our ability to have pure concentration. When removed, there is an allowing of our calm, concentrated, true nature to come through. A brief explanation follows:

The five jhana factors
1. Applied attention.
2. Sustained attention.
3. Joy.
4. Bliss.
5. One-pointedness.

The jhana factors and the hindrances they eliminate
1. Applied attention — calms sense desire.
2. Sustained attention — stops ill will.
3. Joy — eliminates sloth and torpor.
4. Bliss — eliminates restlessness and worry.
5. One-pointedness — overcomes doubt.

Applied attention is the submission of our focus upon the object of meditation. (In our present situation the likely object of meditation is the breath.) By applying our attention directly upon the meditation object, there is no room for sensual desires to be present. To have sensual desires at this time would indicate a lack of sufficient concentration to experience jhana.

Sustained attention is when the attention no longer wavers from the object of meditation. When focusing on the breath, there is a strong and complete connection with the breath without any mental straying. Along with the calming of sense desires comes the stopping of ill will, anger and fear. Applied and sustained attention can be experienced as subtle and separate layers of thought.

Joy (piti) is an exciting or energetic type of happiness. It is a mental joy that is felt within the body in the form of restlessness. This restless joy helps one not to become attached to pleasant feelings. It does this by not allowing us to sustain this feeling for long durations due to its energetic nature. It greatly aids in the elimination of sloth and torpor which is the drowsy or fatigued feeling that can accompany meditation.

Bliss (sukha) is a more refined joy than piti. Bliss can be described as a less physical form of happiness. It is very calming and often follows the restlessness of piti. It is a natural antidote for the redundant mental patterns of worry.

One-pointedness is laser-like, effortless concentration. The attention and focus does not waver from the meditation object. All hindrances, including any doubt in our ability or the practice itself, are no longer present, enabling ones meditation practice to deepen.

There are four jhanas that one can experience. The first of these contains all five of the above jhana factors. As we progress through the jhanas, these factors fall away until we come to the fourth jhana. In the forth jhana, a feeling of equanimity arises as a replacement for bliss (sukha).

Equanimity is a balance of the mind. In jhana this means a unification of consciousness and concentration; a state where there is no influence by sensory input. When reflected upon after the meditation, it could be described as a smooth, steady, and continuous peaceful state of mind.

- First jhana - Applied attention, Sustained attention, Joy, Bliss, One-pointedness.
- Second jhana - Joy, Bliss, One-pointedness.
- Third jhana - Bliss, One-pointedness.
- Fourth jhana - One-pointedness, Equanimity.

Mindfulness of Mind States, #12 Liberating the Mind

"He trains himself, 'Liberating the mind, I shall breathe in.' He trains himself, 'Liberating the mind, I shall breathe out.'"

The Buddha

When the mind is free, it is liberated. This liberation is freedom from attachment to objects, ideals, and past conditioned responses. This is liberation of anything that the mind has been grasping and clinging onto. This may include material possessions such as money, homes, or cars. It can also involve immaterial objects such as opinions and beliefs or theories. Also included are religious activities, and rites and rituals.

The primary aim of liberating the mind from attachment is the letting go of everything that we feel is holding us back from enlightenment. When we contemplate this, we will conclude that trying to call something "mine", or to think "I" own this or that, is a false identity and likely the root of our attachment.

Ultimately, with the mind liberated we can learn to let go of the "thinking mind" altogether. We can develop the ability to rest in the present moment with what is, without allowing thoughts to take us to past or future events and ideas. This happens within the concentrated mind. Liberation of mind is also present within the "clear mind" through insight.

Insight and concentration work as a team. In order to liberate the mind, we must use both for it to be a lasting liberation. It is true that we can liberate the mind through the practice of concentration alone, but this type of liberation will likely fade. Insight can be used in two ways: one is to use it to reflect on the state of the "deeply-concentrated mind". When finished, this will provide a glimpse of the liberation that is possible. Another method to experience the liberated mind is to ask, "What am I holding onto that is preventing me from being free?" Once this profound question is answered, there will be an experience of liberation.

All of this can become even more apparent in the following area of our practice: *Mindfulness of Dhammas*.

Meditation-Concentrating and liberating the mind

Sitting upright and straightening the back, come to a comfortable seated posture. . .

Relax the eyes closed and bring your attention to the breath. . .

Look at the breath as your only object of interest. . .

Ignore any sounds or visualizations . . .

Pay no attention to smells or touch sensations to the skin . . .

Feel the breath at one point on the body. . .

Get to know the place where the breath caresses the body. That one place. . .

Ask yourself, "What is my level of concentration at this moment?". . .

Is there a level of attention that is purposeful and directed?. . .

Can you witness several levels of attention?. . .

Is there a type of attention that has movement and at the same time another type of attention that is stable and sustained?. . .

Is there an absence of sensual desire?. . .

Is there a sensed freedom from ill will, anger and fear?. . .

Is there a noticed lack of thought?. . .

Are there signs of joy and happiness?. . .

Again, ask yourself, "What is my level of concentration at this moment?". . .

Can you come close to an area of no thought?. . .

Is there a sense of mental stillness and freedom from attachment? . . .

Take a few quiet moments and experience the different levels of attention, along with any accumulated joy and bliss. . .

Is there a noticing of one-pointedness, stability, flow, equanimity? . . .

Ask, "What is my level of concentration?" . . .

[Liberating the mind]

With this deep concentration, is there a sense of mental and physical liberation?. . .

Is there a sense of freedom; a sense of letting go?. .

For a few moments, silently connect the words "let go" with the in-and-out breaths. . .

Think "let" with the inhalation and "go" with the exhalation. . .

Can you feel a liberation, or freedom, from wanting and needing?. . .

Is there an absence for the need to move beyond the simple joys of the concentrated mind?. . .

Rest in the peace of concentration. . .

Rest in the liberation from attachment. . .

Freedom from attachment to anything: material, physical or mental. . .

Feel the freedom of the concentrated, liberated mind. . .

Continue for as long as time permits. . . . . .

Mindfulness of Dhammas

In this, the fourth and final tetrad, we work within the heart of Buddhist teachings. Here lies the opportunity for permanent change in the way we view and understand our natural world and who we believe ourselves to be. In this fourth and final group we are using the Dhammas as our meditation object.

Dhamma is a Pali word that has several translations, most of them referring to teaching. The definition by the late Thai monk Buddhadasa Bhikkhu defines Dhamma as "nature, the law and truth of nature, the duty to be performed in accordance with nature, and the results or benefits that arise from the performance of that duty."

Nature has always and will always be our best teacher, and the Buddhist teachings have borrowed from this. The noticing of how life and everything in it is a continuous rising and falling away and how it can be seen as a continual series of birth and death is nature being nature. It is reality.

If nature and its effect are seen and realized beyond a mere intellectual understanding, the experiential understanding that can be witnessed through insight can have a life-altering effect. But yet we seem to try to separate ourselves from nature, perhaps because we think of it in some way being a barbaric lesson in life and death.

These teachings point to the truth that by having or getting something and calling it "I" or "mine" and then expecting these impermanent objects to bring lasting happiness, is how we set ourselves up just to be let down. We do this to ourselves again and again. Impermanence is the true nature of everything. All that we think we have, including our relationships and this body, will have to be given back to nature from where it came; all of it.

Knowing the natural law in this way provides a profound freedom from our habitual way of looking at life and everything in it. We begin to see through the delusion that everything is separate from ourselves and that something can be owned rather than borrowed. In reality, everything is simply the unfolding of life. It is nature fully revealing herself to us and pointing out that everything is a part of nature and is in constant change.

When we study the Dhamma and the mind's reaction to the information it receives from the practice of insight meditation, we realize that we can never come to the point where we can be free from our problems. That is because we already are. We are already free. The freedom and happiness that we seek is found when we realize that there are no problems outside of the mind.

When we come to the place in our practice that we are ready to understand the Dhamma, this information comes in the form of insights; clear knowing that comes from an experiential understanding rather than from mere thought.

In this final area of practice, we will be moving into the area of contemplation. Previously, our emphasis has been on the important aspect of concentration. We will now use the concentration that we have developed, for the purpose of contemplation. Contemplation is the ability to investigate an object beyond the mere ability to think about it. It is the investigative ability of the mind to penetrate into an object's deeper meaning.

All of the sixteen steps in this practice of the Anapanasati are a natural progression. One step can easily follow the next. In the final four steps, this is apparent as we move toward the seeing of unsatisfactoriness for what it is and use this in a wholesome way to understand the impermanence of phenomena and the results of this realization.

Mindfulness of Dhammas, #13 Contemplating Impermanence

"He trains himself, 'Constantly contemplating imperma-nence, I shall breathe in.' He trains himself, 'Constantly contemplating impermanence, I shall breathe out,'"
The Buddha

The fact that everything in our lives is imperma-nent and in constant change is fairly easy to comprehend on an intellectual level, but we mostly go through life without this fact in mind. To know at a continual and deep level that everything in our world, material or immaterial, is in constant change can be a life-changing realization. To deeply pene-trate this understanding, it must include our bodies, our thoughts, all of our possessions and our rela-tionships.

When people first hear this, there is often denial. Upon hearing these words the mind will struggle to find something solid and lasting, such as a soul or some past belief that is contrary to the fact of impermanence. When investigated, we find that in reality it is not that everything is impermanent; it is that impermanence is all that there is.

This impermanence of all things is not negative; in nature, it is actually liberation for us. Knowing that there is nothing whatsoever worth grasping or clinging onto, is freedom. The clear understanding of impermanence saves us a lot of needless suffering.

If all is impermanent, nothing can provide lasting and permanent happiness. Why grasp and cling, or struggle, to obtain anything? This is not to mean that we should not *have*. It means that we should awaken to the fact that it just might not be worth the struggle to obtain that thing or achieve that agenda, just to simply satisfy the part of you that we could call the "self".

With the understanding of impermanence, it becomes a natural part of our behavior to take a moment to consider the consequences of our struggles. If we expect and hope for things to remain the same, including our feelings about possessions, relationships, thoughts etc., we will be let down. This is the suffering that the Buddha was teaching about.

"Behold, O monks, this is my last advice to you. All component things in the world are changeable. They are not lasting. Work hard to gain your own salvation."

These were the final words of the Buddha, spoken prior to his death. Obviously, this enlightened man realized that this understanding was of the upmost importance. Any time we want something and wish for it to remain unchanged, we stand a very real chance of being let down, resulting in stress and suffering.

Mindfulness of Dhammas, #14 Contemplating Fading Away

"He trains himself, 'Constantly contemplating fading away, I shall breathe in.' He trains himself, 'Constantly contemplating fading away, I shall breathe out.'"
The Buddha

Upon the contemplation of impermanence, the natural sequence which follows is the "fading away" of attachment and ultimately the "fading away" of desire. This can be looked at as a natural dissolving of the attachment that we had for the impermanent issues and things that we previously held so precious in life.

We can see this dissolving or fading away when we think of how we once felt toward someone, and how that strong attachment toward him or her has faded away and is no longer present. We can also recall how we wanted something so much that we felt sure that it would make our lives complete. We can think of the child that believes that by having that one toy, life will be forever joyful and not having the toy, will destroy any hopes for a happy life.

Fading away is our realizing that something was a passing and impermanent experience. This dispassionate way of seeing things is a type of wisdom that is similar to the adult that says "no" to the child in the store that wants to have ownership of everything that catches their eye, except the reprimanding is now reflected back toward the self in the form of knowledge.

With fading away, the enchantment with things, people, and places in the material world and the world of the mind is seen through. It becomes an unsatisfactory condition because we can now see the deception and thus the disenchantment or unsatisfactoriness with this deception as it appears. Fading away is a freeing from the pulling effect that things have on us. It is a direct result of our understanding of impermanence. On a deeper level, fading away is seeing through the illusionary view that we have for ourselves. It is seeing through the false ideas that we have build over time about how we believe ourselves to be. This is a fading away of the rigid views we hold regarding how we should present ourselves to others, what we should do with our time, who we are, and what we should have and own. Furthermore, this is a fading away of our attachment to self;

a falling away of the idea that we are separate from the world. It is opposite of the view that we are "here" and that the world is "out there." This is a fading away of our separateness from anything. The result is freedom from wanting things to be different from that which they presently are, which is acceptance, and freedom from the desire for continual change. We are a whole, and it all changes on its own without our help.

We can practice this by examining the state of mind that has become disenchanted with all of the impermanent things and dispassionate with the things that were once desired.

Meditation- Contemplation of impermanence and fading away.

Making yourself comfortable, bring your attention to the breath. . .

Take your time and use the steps that we have learned in the past to calm the mind and body and to balance this calm with the right amount of energy. . .

Using the breath as your focal point, take some time to bring the mind to a state of concentration. . .

Once a decrease of thoughts is apparent, and a gladdening of the mind is noticed, bring your attention to the impermanence of the breath. . .

Notice the beginning and the passing away of each breath. . .

Notice how each breath is different than the last one; each breath beginning and then ending. . .

See the impermanence in each breath. . .

See impermanence in each thought . . .

See the thoughts come and go. . .

See the impermanence in each action and everything that is perceived, and in each visualization . . .

See the impermanence in each moment of time: each minute, each hour, each day. . .

See the impermanence in the passing months, in the passing years, in the passing lives. . .

[fading away]

Ask, "What does impermanence mean to me?". . .

Is there sadness? . . .

Is there a feeling of relief?. . .

Is there a deeper understanding of your position in life? . . .

Can you see that suffering and stress come from wanting more, or wanting less, of all these impermanent things? . . .

Can you see that freedom from this suffering and stress is simply the understanding of impermanence at a deeper level? . . .

Visualize a fading away of all attachments. . .

How would it feel to be free from all attachments in life? . . .

Can you get a sense of the freedom felt from letting go and allowing this fading away to take place?. . .

Can you take this practice with you in life? . . .

Continue for as long as time permits. . . . .

Mindfulness of Dhammas, #15 Contemplating Cessation

"He trains himself, 'Constantly contemplating cessation, I shall breathe in.' He trains himself, 'Constantly contemplating cessation, I shall breathe out.'"
The Buddha

With the extinction and fading away of attachment comes the cessation of suffering itself. With the cessation of suffering, the mind is very clear and is free from all of the symptoms of attachment. It is only from this place of freedom that we can see and understand how we were truly held captive by the mind. This can be realized within four areas of our lives; four kinds of freedom found through the cessation of suffering.

There is freedom from the suffering and fear of birth, aging, sickness and death. This fear is a direct result of our attachment to our body; those things accumulated mentally. This brings about the fear that we have something to lose. In reality, we have never truly been in charge of, or the owner, of this body. If we were truly the owners, we could stop the body from aging and from experiencing sickness. It is more of a fact that we are borrowing the form we have. This is much like a coat that can be worn. If we have an old coat, when finished with its use, we discard it and forget about it. Can we do the same with the body and mind?

There is freedom from the conditions of suffering: pain, sorrow, sadness, and despair. This pain and sadness that can be felt, is due to the feeling that it is "I" who is feeling this. This is due to the identification and the "story" we place behind the feelings and thoughts.

There is freedom from the wants and desires to be for or against agreeable and disagreeable things. Freedom from having everything the way in which you would like them is the understanding that we cannot take anything with us at the end of this life. Our world is very material. In this way of looking, all things are simply experienced.

Finally, there is cessation of suffering based on the freedom of the view that we are any of the five aggregates. The five aggregates are the accumulation of things that we habitually think of as "me". These are: form (body), feelings, perceptions, thoughts, and sense consciousness (mind).

When these five aspects are seen through, we then find a cessation to suffering. The realization of this step is very important. It is the realization of our selfless nature. With the realization of the selfless nature, we no longer claim anything as being "I" or "mine". Once the self or ego is seen through and identified as being false, there is cessation of suffering. This comes about due to the absence of there being anyone to suffer. As this happens, there is the understanding that all of the wants and desires we previously had were a continuous wanting for more of this or less of that. This wanting is the result of a continual lack of contentment or fulfillment for the self. Additionally, this lack of contentment is a by-product of the same desire that had been searched for all along. This can be seen as an ugly contentment–desire–contentment–desire type of feedback loop and is brought about by the impermanent nature of all desires and the quest for the fulfillment one thinks they will provide.

Our selfless nature is the result of seeing that nothing is worth cling to because it is impermanent and cannot provide lasting happiness. Eventually, all is seen as selfless, resulting in the cessation of suffering.

Mindfulness of Dhammas, #16 Contemplating Relinquishment

"He trains himself, 'Constantly contemplating relinquishment, I shall breathe in.' He trains himself, 'Constantly contemplating relinquishment, I shall breathe out.'"

The Buddha

In this final step, Contemplating Relinquishment, we find a "throwing back" or a "giving back" to where it all came from. It can also be seen as a giving up of the idea that we are, or can be, in control of or own anything. We can penetrate through these false ideas by using contemplation and insight.

As previously mentioned, it is the idea of the "self" that gives us the feeling that we can have ownership. Through contemplation, we will find that in the shadows of this ownership, there is always a hope for the fulfillment of being in control of the thing being owned or that it will, in some way, place us in a position where we are more in control of our lives.

We have borrowed from nature in a way that we feel we are "above it all" and that nature is there simply to be a provider for us. We may likely feel like nature is, "out there," as if it is separate from us. It is as if we can leave our home and go out into nature. Although with close examination, we will find that we cannot go out into nature because we are nature.

Nature has an incredible ability to "take back". Dead wood will decay and slowly return to the soil; metal will rust and oxidize returning to nature from where it came. Our used up bodies will decompose and return to the soil as well. In all, everything that we have ever used will eventually return to its original state.

It is through the realization of impermanence and the relinquishment of attachment that we realize that we cannot truly be in control of anything in this world. Everything rises and falls and then away from awareness and returns from where it came. Even our thoughts freely come and go, sometimes at various frequencies and different levels, but still uncontrolled.

If we had control, we would be god-like in all of our endeavors. Our environment and lives would be perfect, our bodies and health would be perfect, and all of us would most certainly be enlightened.

The ultimate practice is to see all things without attachment. We are to contemplate the truth of Dhamma in everything until there is no attachment left. We are to see all material, physical, and mental phenomena including our form, the body, as a part of the passing experience of life.

It is through the understanding of impermanence, and the fading away of attachment through the cessation of suffering, that we can finally relinquish our view of the self and can truly be free from the suffering that is caused by our need to control, and our attachment to the fulfillment of the self.

Meditation-A contemplation of cessation and relinquishment

Sit comfortably. . .

With the eyes closed and the body comfortable, bring your focus to the breath. . .

Experience the long and short breaths. . .
Bring your attention to your breathing as it conditions the body. . .

Experience the breath and any feelings associated with the breath. . .

Allow the breath to soften. . .

Feel a state of concentration taking hold. . .

Notice your posture, your energy, and your current feelings and ask, "What mind state is currently being noticed?". . .

See it all as simply a moment in time. . .

See the impermanence in all of it. . .

Keep the breath smooth and flowing. . .

Ask, "Is there anything worth hanging onto if it is all momentary?". . .

Is attachment necessary? . . .

What is freedom from attachment? . . .

How does it feel to realize that there is nothing worth hanging onto and no one to do the hanging on? . . .

Imagine the peacefulness found in no longer having to defend or protect property or ideas. . .

What is the experience of being free from hanging onto anything? Complete freedom from attachment? . . .

Freedom from the self?. . .

Imagine a messenger that has bad news to deliver, but there is no one available to receive this bad news. . .

Desperately looking but unable to find anyone to deliver the bad news to, the messenger becomes exhausted. . .

Giving up the pursuit, the messenger writes the bad news on paper, nails it to a post and leaves. . .

Still, no one is there to read the news. . .

Eventually, wind and rain destroy the paper and the bad news is destroyed as well. . .

In the same way, imagine there is no self to receive negativity. . .

There is no "you" to receive negativity, restlessness, or worry. . .

Relinquishment of all conditioned things, including the self, is giving up the need to identify with anything. . .

See yourself looking out through a window of a building. . .

Bring your attention to the sights of nature that lie just outside this building. . .

Notice any feelings of separateness that you may feel with the things you see outside the window. . .

You are seeing plants and small animals through the window. You see the open sky and the movement of the leaves on the trees as the wind lightly blows. . .

Now imagine the window and the wall from which you are looking being removed and vanishing. . .

Notice that there is no longer any separation between you and the natural world . . .

Now see you, as a part of nature; as one with everything; no longer separate. . .

Nature no longer being "out there"; all things being a part of your world and awareness. . .

All things a part of the whole; a part of and connected through nature. . .

Everything that we have ever owned, in reality, cannot be possessed. . .

All that we have ever thought of owning, or felt that we owned, is simply borrowed. . .

Look back at the possessions you had as a child; all gone. . .

Look back at every piece of food you have ever
tasted; all returned. . .

Look back at the possessions that all deceased
people thought they owned; all returned. . .

All things return to the source, all objects return to
nature. . .

See all as impermanent. See all without attachment,
and see all things without the label of self. . . .

Continue for as long as time permits. . . . . .

The Heart of the Practice

When we sit down to meditate, we can notice many things within the body and mind taking place. This is due to the fact that we are taking the time to sit down and notice these things. We will notice things like: how busy the mind is with thoughts, and how uncomfortable the body can become, and feelings of fatigue, boredom, pain and anxiety. We may also notice energy, contentment and serenity.

If we look at our meditation practices as a representation of our lives, as the understanding of all that we are, we can easily learn the value of the practice and gain a clear picture of the true purpose behind it.

The knowing that our silent time, the time we set aside for meditation, is simply a time to get a clear look at ourselves can be a profound period of self-discovery. As we see the activity of the mind, we are getting a clear look at life and not seeing the thoughts and mental activity as being us but the one who is watching this activity.

Any improvements in or during our meditation can be looked at as improvements in our life, and this is done through concentration and reflection, which results in insight. So, we are what and how we meditate. If we notice tension in the body and then use the long breath to relax and counteract this tension, we are taking control of the situation in a positive manner. If we learn to use the energizing short breath to combat fatigue and stabilize our posture, we are using mindfulness to notice and then properly utilize the breath.

Through concentration and more importantly knowing when we are concentrated, we can deeply penetrate into the sensations and feelings that are such a big part of us. The control of our reactions to feelings is, in a large way, the control over our lives. Our continuous movement toward the things that we *feel* we need to make us happy or our moving away from the things that we *feel* we must avoid can cause unpleasantness in our life. Meditation can allow us to understand that we can simply watch all of this activity without reacting to it. We also learn that it is through concentration that the feelings lose their grip on us. This allows a true form of happiness to take its place; a happiness that is born from serenity. This is a serenity that comes from the calming of the push and pull of feelings.

Our mind states, or states of mind, are an invaluable area to learn and understand through our practice of meditation. When in meditation, we can simply investigate and momentarily witness the state of mind that presently resides. Although very temporary, this points out another aspect of us. What state are we in at this moment and why? Can we see it change, and how are the ways it changes? What does deep concentration do to depression? What does the identification of a mind state instantly do to the state itself?

The understanding of the nature of reality is, for many, the reason behind the meditation practices. This is the dhamma; the understanding of impermanence and the way in which all things are connected and interrelate. This is the practice of insight; an investigation of our reaction to phenomena. It is a type of contemplation that utilizes the aspect of concentration. It starts with the mental penetration into impermanence, which results in the clear comprehension of why suffering and stress are linked to our trying to save and hold onto that which is impermanent and ever-changing. Through our practice, we can learn to see through the idea that we must hang onto anything in order to be complete. We can learn to see this in ourselves, in others, and in all worldly things, including places and events.

Our formal meditation practice is an opportunity for us to witness our own lives at a deeper level than we can when we are out in the world. It is a moment in our day when we can sit on the wayside and watch as the world, in the form of thoughts, feelings, and their results, moves about without our being involved. It is through this simple act of watching that we learn and understand life. How we react to our experiences during our meditation practice points directly to whom and what we are in our life beyond meditation. This cannot be denied.

If we cannot sit and be with ourselves in silence for a specified time each day, we must ask ourselves why and take a deep look at our life and our true purpose for being here. We must never forget that what we see during our meditation practice, and on the way to or away from the practice, is who we are.

In Summary

We have passed through the areas of body and mind within these practices of *mindfulness with breathing*: "The Anapanasati Sutta". Once familiar with the Sutta and the sixteen different areas, you may have found that you were drawn to one or more particular areas of the Sutta.

Until you become well familiar with each area of the sixteen areas of *mindfulness with breathing*, it is advised that you work through each area in sequence from one to sixteen. Once you become familiar with them, you may likely find that for some reason, a particular area may seem to apply to your practice of meditation at any given time. It may seem to make more sense or be clearer than the other areas, or it may just seem easier to work with. Whatever the reason, one should feel free to experiment and work with these areas of *mindfulness with breathing* and find which one, or ones, suit you the best at any particular time.

The practice of meditation is meant to provide us with methods to look within; to see what is happening within the body, feelings, mind states and the Dhammas. As our meditation becomes more refined and developed, we will notice a clarity of thought, and insights will arise that can help point the way to a happier and less stressful existence for those with whom you live and associate.

The key is consistency in the practice. The length of time one spends practicing meditation is important, but the frequency of the practice is essential. One should practice daily. It is suggested that you start your practice with twenty minutes each day, and then once you notice the benefits, begin to lengthen the time. This is likely to happen unconsciously.

A little tip: always consider remaining in the meditation posture for approximately five minutes longer than your scheduled meditation time. After your meditation time is finished, spend these five minutes to review what was done and how you feel about the practice. This will often be the best part of your meditation. It is a "letting go" of any kind of time restraints or ritual in the meditation practice and a simple acceptance of "what is".

Continual Breath Awareness

The breath is by far the most common meditation object and rightly so because it is always with us. We can have nothing in this world and still own the most useful meditation tool known to man, the breath. Typically, we may use the breath during our meditation practice, and once we are finished with the practice, we discard the breath and go about our day, never giving our old friend, the breath, another thought until we are either back in meditation or have difficulty breathing for some reason.

Continual breath awareness allows us to control the many thousands of needless thoughts we have each day. By grounding our awareness, we can still notice the thoughts, but this noticing is different than the actual thinking of the thoughts. With *continual breath awareness*, there is no zoning out, as with dullness, and there is no being carried away with the thinking mind, so we can still easily function within the world.

With the mindfulness and awareness that is brought about by *continual breath awareness*, we have the freedom to investigate thoughts without judgment whenever we choose to do so. This is much different than allowing the thoughts to control our minds and our world.

The entire practice of *continual breath awareness* is based on the ability to develop a relationship with the breath throughout the day. There must be a desire to stay connected with the breath, both in formal meditation and when you are not in formal meditation. In other words, when you are out in the world doing what you do.

When we practice *continual breath awareness*, we find that our level of attention on the breath varies. It may be very good and strong in the beginning, and then it gets weak. Maybe you feel it as being light but consistent, say 40% concentration, or strong and powerful, maybe 80-90%. Every time we evaluate this percentage in this way we are being mindful and develop stronger concentration and mindfulness. We control our thoughts; the thinking process slows down. We develop a deep understanding with regard to our concentration abilities. We learn that our awareness can only hold onto one object at a time.

Ultimately, by practicing *continual Breath awareness*, we become happier. When we increase our awareness and understanding, we will be continuously aware of the fact that our joy and happiness are simply a choice. There is nothing out there that can make us unhappy. Our difficulties come from inside. The world does not have to be at peace with you, but you can be at peace with the world.

Continual breath awareness is a practice where you place your attention on the breath throughout the day and watch what happens. It is mindfulness, concentration, tranquility, inner wisdom, and a true liberation from stress and suffering. It is a form of constant meditation.

Continual breath awareness is mentioned here, because it correlates directly with the practice of "Anapanasati" *mindfulness of breathing,* as well as other spiritual teachings and doctrines that incorporate meditation or "going within" in their systems of practice. It uses the breath in conjunction with the body, physical and mental feelings, the mind states or emotions, and it can be practiced at all times.

We can start by simply and slowly expanding the duration of time we stay on the breath. It can take days, weeks, years, or lifetimes to be fully "awakened", but the benefits of the practice we do to get there are noticed immediately. Try carrying the breath with you always and experience the results for yourself.

"May all beings happily discover their true nature,
and may all beings benefit by these practices"

Author's Biography

 Shane Wilson is an ordained minister in the Buddhist tradition. He trained in Thailand and the United States, and has practiced and studied various meditation techniques throughout the world. In 2001, he founded the Meditation Learning Center in Mesa, Arizona. He regularly teaches meditation and conducts retreats, workshops, classes and seminars worldwide. He is the author of "Meditation, The Great Teacher".

Visit him on the web at:
www.meditationlearningcenter.com
And at:
www.shanewilson.org

CPSIA information can be obtained at www.ICGtesting.com
Printed in the USA
LVOW092155130212

268563LV00006B/44/P